NBA FUN FACTS AND TRIVIA

NBA FUN FACTS AND TRIVIA

BY HOWARD BLATT

SCHOLASTIC INC.
New York   Toronto   London   Auckland   Sydney

If you purchased this book without a cover, you should be aware that this book is stolen property. It was reported as "unsold and destroyed" to the publisher, and neither the author nor the publisher has received payment for this "stripped book."

No part of this publication may be reproduced in whole or in part, or stored in a retrieval system, or transmitted in any form or by any means, electronic, mechanical, photocopying, recording, or otherwise, without written permission of the publisher. For information regarding permission, write to Scholastic Inc.,
555 Broadway, New York, NY 10012.

The NBA and individual NBA member team identifications are trademarks, copyrighted designs and other forms of intellectual property of NBA Properties, Inc. and the respective member teams and may not be used without the prior written consent of NBA Properties, Inc. All rights reserved.

ISBN 0-590-03271-2

© 1998 by NBA Properties, Inc.
All rights reserved. Published by Scholastic Inc.

24 23 22 21 20 19 18 17 16 15 14   6 7 8 9/0

Printed in the U.S.A.
First Scholastic printing, July 1998
Book design: Michael Malone

MICHAEL ARRIVES

The game most people recall as the one in which Michael Jordan gave notice to the NBA that he was playing in a league that included only himself came during the playoffs after his second pro season.

His Airness had missed all but 18 games of the regular campaign with a foot injury. However, on April 20, 1986, playing in front of a hostile Boston Garden crowd in Game 2 of what became a first-round Celtic sweep, Jordan erased Elgin Baylor's NBA playoff record of 61 points by scoring 63 during Chicago's 135–131 double-overtime defeat.

Even though Jordan missed an open 15-footer at the end of the first overtime that would've given the Bulls the victory, his performance was astounding enough to prompt Celtic Larry Bird to observe, "I think it was God disguised as Michael Jordan."

The breakdown of Mike's assault from the floor was: 13 jumpers, seven drives, one follow-up, one goaltended stationary layup and one dunk.

BEST SHOT-BLOCKERS (career)

Hakeem Olajuwon	3,363
Kareem Abdul-Jabbar	3,189
Mark Eaton	3,064
Tree Rollins	2,542
Patrick Ewing	2,516

> Please note that all the stats documented in this book are NBA totals only (no ABA stats included) and do not include the 1997–98 season.

DON'T GET INTO THEIR KITCHEN

The following NBA players, past and present, have names that just might make your mouth water.

Glen Rice
Dell Curry
Michael Curry
Will Perdue
Darvin Ham
Greg Graham
Elden Campbell
Clarence (Spoon) Weatherspoon
Darwin Cook
Jeff Cook
Mark Eaton
Bernie Fryer
Billy (The Whopper) Paultz
Vin Baker

Who is the oldest player to appear in an NBA game?

A. Kareem Abdul-Jabbar
B. John Long
C. Bob Cousy
D. Robert Parish
E. Herb Williams

ANSWER: Robert Parish played for a record 21 seasons before retiring at age 43 following the 1996–97 season when he played for the Chicago Bulls.

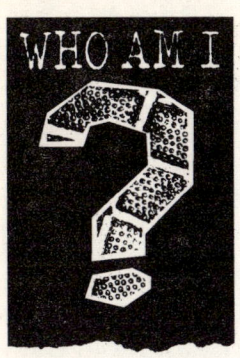

WHO AM I

- Born July 23, 1968, I honed my toughness and my game on the Oakland playgrounds, modeling myself after boyhood hero George Gervin.

- I was the No. 2 overall pick in the 1990 NBA Draft, as Oregon State's all-time leading scorer.

- I have posted career highs of 38 points, 17 assists, 12 rebounds and 8 steals.

- I improved my scoring average for four straight seasons, from 7.2 points per game as a rookie in 1990–91 to 20.6 in 1994–95.

- My defensive skills have earned me the nickname "The Glove."

- I led the NBA in steals with a career-high average of 2.85 in 1995–96 and was named NBA Defensive Player of the Year.

- I have a reputation as the owner of the quickest feet, hands and tongue in the West.

ANSWER: MY NAME IS GARY PAYTON.

JUST MAGIC

On February 9, 1992, a crowd of 14,272 at Orlando Arena and a curious national TV audience found themselves riveted by a remarkable tour de force that turned an ensemble exhibition into a memorable one-man Magic show.

On an All-Star stage befitting his greatness, Earvin Johnson responded to the worries and the doubts from his many fans. It had been three months and four days since Johnson had dropped his sudden bombshell that ended his amazing NBA career with the Los Angeles Lakers, in the wake of being diagnosed with the HIV virus that often leads to AIDS.

But remarkably, Magic looked like he had never been away from the court, notching 25 points and nine assists and the Most Valuable Player award in the West's 153–113 victory over the East.

Within the last 90 seconds, Johnson hit West All-Star teammate Dan Majerle with a no-look pass for a backdoor layup, challenged and made defensive stops on Isiah Thomas and Michael Jordan on isolation plays and then provided the capper to his masterpiece. Magic drilled what seemed to be a wild, flat-footed, three-point shot from four feet beyond the arc—his third trey within the final three minutes.

Although 14.5 seconds were left, nobody was playing anymore. There was too much hugging going on. Game called on account of love.

BEST THREE-POINT SHOOTERS
(career, minimum 250 made)

Player	FGM	FGA	.PCT
Steve Kerr	520	1,091	.477
Drazen Petrovic	255	583	.437
B. J. Armstrong	407	947	.430
Hubert Davis	333	776	.429
Dana Barros	799	1,926	.415

Bryant Stith's middle name is Lamonica, after former Oakland Raiders quarterback Daryle Lamonica.

GOING TOGETHER LIKE PICK AND ROLL

Consider these pairs of NBA name pairs, past and present:

Todd Day/Travis Knight
Alonzo Mourning/Brevin Knight
Priest Lauderdale/God Shammgod
Chris Childs/Greg Minor
J. R. Reid/Sharone Wright
Don Reid/Lorenzen Wright
Donyell Marshall/Charles Outlaw
Jason Kidd/Derek Grimm
Blue Edwards/Ed Gray
Purvis Short/Grant Long
Rolando Blackman/Donald Whiteside
World B. Free/Michael Cage

WHO AM I

- Born in Memphis, Tennessee, I was raised to avoid the temptations of the streets by my grandmother, who gave me my nickname.

- I overcame an injury from a bullet in the foot sustained during a robbery to have a sensational college career, and I became the second All-American ever to play at Memphis State, joining Keith Lee.

- I came to Orlando from the Golden State Warriors in a Draft Day deal for No. 1 overall pick Chris Webber and three No. 1 picks prior to the 1993–94 season.

- Because of my 6-foot-7 height and my versatility as a playmaker and a scorer, I have been compared to Magic Johnson—by Magic himself.

- I was named to the All-NBA First Team in my second pro season, in 1994–95, averaging 20.9 points, 7.2 assists, 4.4 rebounds and 1.69 steals.

- I scored 42 and 41 points in back-to-back playoff games against Miami, April 29 and May 1, 1997, becoming the first player ever to notch 40 or more in consecutive games against a Pat Riley-coached team.

- I was switched from point guard to off guard by new coach Chuck Daly in 1997–98.

ANSWER: MY NAME IS ANFERNEE HARDAWAY.

MICHAEL RETURNS

It is true that Michael Jordan's all-time single-game high was a 69-point effort against the Cleveland Cavaliers, March 28, 1990. However, the Jordan explosion most remarkable for its complete unpredictability came on the fifth anniversary of that performance, in his fifth game and his 11th day back following a mid-season return from a season-plus retirement.

Weeks removed from failing to handle Double-A curves in Birmingham, Michael figured to still be shedding cobwebs from his game. He could not possibly be in top basketball shape. Nevertheless, Jordan came into New York's Madison Square Garden and rang up 55 points—more points than anyone had scored since the new building had opened in 1968.

Dunking only once, he unveiled his new persona as the silkiest of long-range jump shooters and eluded six different defenders en route to 21–of–37 from the floor in just 39 minutes. Jordan made nine of his first 11 for 20 first-quarter points on his way to 35 for the first half.

Finally, with the score tied at 111 and all 55 Jordan points already on the board, Michael drove to the right elbow of the foul line, drew the double team from Patrick Ewing and John Starks—and found a wide-open Bill Wennington for the game-winning slam with 3.1 seconds left.

Any questions?

Blue Edwards got his nickname from his older sister, who once found him choking while he was a baby.

GREATEST SCORING GAMES IN NBA PLAYOFF HISTORY

Player	Points	Date
Michael Jordan	63	4/20/86
Elgin Baylor	61	4/14/62
Wilt Chamberlain	56	3/22/62
Michael Jordan	56	4/2/92
Charles Barkley	56	5/4/94
Rick Barry	55	4/18/67
Michael Jordan	55	5/1/88
Michael Jordan	55	6/16/93
Michael Jordan	55	4/27/97
John Havlicek	54	4/1/73
Michael Jordan	54	5/31/93

The team with the longest winning streak in NBA history, with 33 games in a row is:

A. the 1969–70 New York Knicks
B. the 1970–71 Milwaukee Bucks
C. the 1972–73 Philadelphia 76ers
D. the 1971–72 Los Angeles Lakers
E. the 1995–96 Chicago Bulls

ANSWER: The 1971–72 Los Angeles Lakers—with Wilt Chamberlain, Jerry West and Elgin Baylor—ran off 33 in a row.

Greg Anderson has been known as "Cadillac" since his college days as a freshman at the University of Houston, when a bike was his primary mode of transportation.

DEFENSE TAKES A HOLIDAY

They went up and down the court and filled the lanes and filled the baskets until you expected the nets to combust.

In three overtimes, the Detroit Pistons defeated the Denver Nuggets, 186–184, at Denver's McNichols Arena, December 13, 1983, in the highest-scoring game in NBA history.

The Nuggets' Kiki Vandeweghe led all scorers with 51 points on 21-of-29 shooting from the floor, while teammate Alex English managed 48. For the winners, Isiah Thomas notched 47, John Long had 41 and Kelly Tripucka had 35.

As a team, the Nuggets shot .591 for the game while Detroit finished the night at .544. The score was tied at 145 at the end of regulation, at 159 at the end of the first OT, at 171 the end of the second.

Compare that wild one with the one at the other end of the NBA spectrum—the league's lowest-scoring game. The Fort Wayne Pistons defeated the Minneapolis Lakers, 19–18, in Minneapolis, November 22, 1950, long before the advent of the 24-second clock.

In that contest, franchise center George Mikan wound up with 15 of the Lakers' 18 points and all four of their field goals. John Oldham was Fort Wayne's high scorer with five points. There was a total of 31 shots taken from the floor, by both teams.

WHO AM I

- Born October 5, 1972, in Dallas, I am the son of a nationally known sports star.

- Duke won NCAA championships in my freshman and sophomore seasons and went to the Finals when I was a senior.

- I was drafted No. 3 overall in 1994, behind Milwaukee's Glenn Robinson and Dallas' Jason Kidd.

- My dad Calvin is a former Dallas Cowboys running back great, and my mom Janet is an attorney and a former Wellesley College suitemate of Hillary Rodham Clinton.

- I became the 15th player in NBA history to lead my team in points, rebounds and assists in 1995–96 and did it again in 1996–97.

- I am a Piston perfectly suited to playing in Motown, because I am an accomplished pianist, even though my niche is classical.

- I became the first NBA rookie to lead the league in the All-Star voting (1,289,585) and the NBA co-Rookie of the Year in 1994–95.

ANSWER: MY NAME IS GRANT HILL.

YOU CAN CALL HIM DIKE

Dikembe Mutombo, who was born in Kinshasa, Congo(Zaire), has a hard time fitting his full name on his driver's license: Dikembe Mutomo Mpolondo Mukamba Jean Jacque Wamutombo. That is a mouthful in any of the many languages that the Hawks' center can speak (English, French, Portuguese, Spanish and five African dialects).

Which of the following players was drafted ahead of Michael Jordan in 1984?

A. Charles Barkley
B. Sam Bowie
C. Sam Perkins
D. Patrick Ewing
E. Karl Malone

ANSWER: Sam Bowie, a 7-foot center from Kentucky whose NBA career was damaged by a series of severe leg injuries, was taken second overall by the Portland Trail Blazers in 1984, after the Houston Rockets had drafted Hakeem Olajuwon from the University of Houston. The Chicago Bulls had to settle for North Carolina's Michael Jordan with the third pick.

> **Knick draft pick Charlie Ward was a Heisman Trophy winner as a quarterback at Florida State, but was not drafted by an NFL team. Though he did not play baseball in college, he was also drafted by the Milwaukee Brewers in 1993.**

CAPTAIN WILLIS IGNITES KNICKS

The crowd at Madison Square Garden buzzed with worry as the Knicks took the court in the minutes prior to Game 7 of the NBA Finals against Wilt Chamberlain and the Los Angeles Lakers, May 8, 1970.

Would Willis Reed be able to play?

The Knicks faithful did not spot their team's captain, center and heart, who had injured a leg in Game 5 and had missed the Knicks' Game 6 loss.

Minutes later, however, a roar went up. The crowd had spotted Reed limping down the tunnel alone, dressed to do battle, coming from the locker room where he had just received two cortisone injections so he could attempt to play. The deafening din continued as Willis gingerly threw up his practice shots and again when his name was announced as a starter.

Riding the emotional lift that he had given to his team, Reed somehow managed to hit two jumpers off his one healthy leg in the opening minutes for a 4–0 Knick lead—before it quickly became clear that he could barely move.

Walt Frazier took over the leadership from there, with 36 points and 19 assists. But Reed had provided the Knicks with the inspiration that led to a 113–99 victory and the first title in franchise history.

Christian Laettner was named after Christian Diestl, a German soldier played by Marlon Brando in the film *The Young Lions*.

THE BOTTOM-DOLLAR TEAM

The following NBA players are/were deserving of top billing.

(Dollar) Bill Bradley
Mark Price
Buck Williams
Penny Hardaway
Gene Banks
Gail Goodrich
Harvey Grant
A. C. Green
Eric Money

> Michael Jordan says the player in NBA history whom he would most like to play one-on-one is Jerry West.

TOP-10 CAREER SCORERS
(by average, minimum 400 games or 10,000 points)

Player	Total Points	Average
Michael Jordan	26,920	31.7
Wilt Chamberlain	31,419	30.1
Elgin Baylor	23,149	27.4
Jerry West	25,192	27.0
Bob Pettit	20,880	26.4
George Gervin	20,708	26.2
Karl Malone	25,592	26.1
Oscar Robertson	26,710	25.7
David Robinson	14,366	25.5
Dominique Wilkins	26,534	25.3

BIRD LENDS A LAST-SECOND HAND

Larry Bird was always fond of saying, like some basketball version of Yogi Berra, "When there's time left, there is always a chance."

The Celtics franchise forward proved the wisdom in that sentiment in Game 5 of the Eastern Conference Finals against the Detroit Pistons at the Boston Garden, May 26, 1987.

With Boston down one and five seconds left, Bird somehow anticipated and swiped an inbounds pass from Isiah Thomas. Then, Larry found a cutting Dennis Johnson with a pass for an assist on the difficult backhand layup that gave the Celtics a 108–107 victory and a three-games-to-two series lead en route to a seven-game conquest.

BEST FREE THROW SHOOTERS
(career, minimum 1,200 made)

Player	FTM	FTA	PCT.
Mark Price	2,048	2,259	.907
Rick Barry	3,818	4,243	.900
Calvin Murphy	3,445	3,864	.892
Scott Skiles	1,548	1,741	.889
Larry Bird	3,960	4,471	.886

> Brian Grant is called "The General" because General Ulysses S. Grant resided in his hometown of Georgetown, Ohio, from 1823 to 1839.

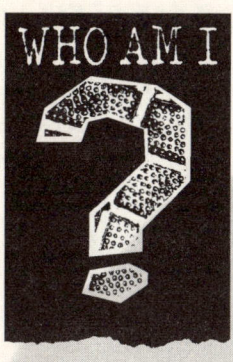

WHO AM I

- Born March 26, 1962, in Spokane, Washington, I grew up pretending I was Sonics' superstar guard Gus Williams.

- A late bloomer, I was drafted a measly 16th overall in 1984, out of little Gonzaga University, where my grandfather had been an All-American triple-threat halfback in 1924.

- Cut from the 1984 U.S. Olympic Team by Bobby Knight, I was a member of the 1992 and 1996 Dream Teams.

- I played in a remarkable 608 consecutive NBA games before missing the start of 1997–98 because of knee surgery, and I missed just four games over my first 13 pro seasons in Utah.

- I share the single-game playoff record for assists with Magic Johnson, notching 24 vs. the Lakers, May 17, 1988.

- I am the career leader in all-time steals, passing Maurice Cheeks, now at 2,531 and counting.

- I am also the career leader in all-time assists, passing Magic Johnson, now at 12,170 and counting.

ANSWER: MY NAME IS JOHN STOCKTON.

BIRD, 'NIQUE SHOOT LIGHTS OUT

The folks lucky enough to be in Boston Garden that day are still talking about the duel between scoring machines. How often do two great shooters at the height of their power go toe-to-toe? But that is the way it happened for Larry Bird and Dominique Wilkins in the fourth quarter of Game 7 of the Eastern Conference semifinals, May 22, 1988.

Wilkins wound up winning the point battle, 47–34, but Bird made sure the Celtics won the war by surviving Dominique's Atlanta Hawks, 118–116. In the final period, each team converted 17 of 20 field-goal attempts. In their can-you-top-this engagement, Bird made nine of his 10 fourth-quarter shots for 20 points while Wilkins notched 16 points over the final 12 minutes.

"Like the Shootout at the O.K. Corral," said Bird's teammate Reggie Lewis.

"The basket was like a well," said Wilkins. "I couldn't miss. He couldn't miss."

And we can't forget it.

> Horace Grant, who teams with his twin brother, Harvey, to form the highest rebounding brother tandem in NBA history (9,774 entering 1997–98), was born nine minutes ahead of Harvey.

MATCHES MADE IN HEAVEN

Match the famous guard-forward and guard-center tandems.

Magic Johnson	Scottie Pippen
Guy Rodgers	Elgin Baylor
Bob Cousy	Wilt Chamberlain
John Stockton	Karl Malone
Mark Price	Brad Daugherty
Jerry West	Bill Russell
Walt Frazier	Julius Erving
Maurice Cheeks	Willis Reed
Michael Jordan	Kareem Abdul-Jabbar

ANSWERS: Magic Johnson/Kareem Abdul-Jabbar; Guy Rodgers/Wilt Chamberlain; Bob Cousy/Bill Russell; John Stockton/Karl Malone; Mark Price/Brad Daugherty; Jerry West/Elgin Baylor; Walt Frazier/Willis Reed; Maurice Cheeks/Julius Erving; Michael Jordan/Scottie Pippen

What number did Michael Jordan wear when he returned to the Bulls during the 1994–95 season?

A. 00
B. 33
C. 23
D. 45
E. He had no number, just a symbol that stood for The Hoop Legend Known as Air.

ANSWER: Jordan abandoned his usual No. 23 to return in 45, the same number he wore as a minor league baseball player for the Birmingham Barons.

THE SHOT HEARD 'ROUND CLEVELAND

It is known simply as "The Shot" in both Chicago and Cleveland.

The Cavaliers led the fifth and deciding game of their first-round Eastern Conference playoff series against the Bulls, 100–99, and the Cleveland fans were whooping it up in anticipation of a title run, May 7, 1989.

However, Chicago had one more trick up its sleeve—an unfathomable, unstoppa-Bull magician named Michael Jordan. Jordan drove to just inside the top of the key then, falling away from the basket to his left, shot a bullet through the cords and into the Cavaliers' hearts from 18 feet, over a lunging Craig Ehlo's extended fingertips.

Chicago won the game, 101–100, and went to the Eastern Finals. It was certainly not the last time that Jordan would save his team by making an impossible shot with all the money on the table.

> David Thompson and George Gervin went into their final games of the 1977–78 season, dueling for the NBA scoring title. Thompson scored 73 in the afternoon—the most ever scored in an NBA game by someone not named Wilt Chamberlain. Gervin, needing 58 points that night to finish No. 1, got 63—including 33 in a single quarter.

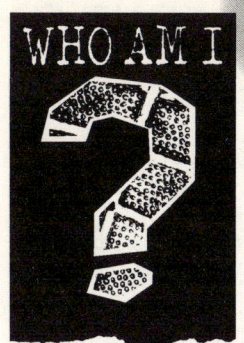

WHO AM I

- On November 4, 1996, I became the fourth player in NBA history to exceed 20,000 points, 10,000 rebounds and 3,500 assists.

- I was cut from the 1984 Olympic Team and had to wait until 1992 and 1996 to earn my gold medals.

- I played eight seasons in Philadelphia, inheriting the mantle as the Sixers' superstar player from Julius Erving after three seasons of playing alongside him.

- An 11-time All-Star through 1996–97, I was named one of the 50 Greatest Players in NBA History.

- I was NBA MVP in 1992–93, when I averaged 25.6 points and 12.2 rebounds and collected six triple-doubles, while leading the Phoenix Suns to the best record in the league.

- Going into 1997–98, I had a string of 11 straight seasons in which I averaged at least 20 points and 10 rebounds.

- I have been traded twice in my NBA career, for three players (from Philly to Phoenix for Jeff Hornacek, Andrew Lang and Tim Perry) in 1992 and four players (from Phoenix to Houston for Robert Horry, Sam Cassell, Chucky Brown and Mark Bryant) in 1996.

ANSWER:
MY NAME IS CHARLES BARKLEY.

WORKING OVERTIME — FOUR OTs

The Phoenix Suns and the Portland Trail Blazers became the eighth set of NBA teams to hook up for a four-overtime game, November 14, 1997—the first such marathon of its kind since 1987. And the fans lucky enough to be on hand for the classic struggle at Portland's Rose Garden were not the only ones to appreciate a night to remember.

"This was the kind of game you live for," said the Blazers' Brian Grant, who played an incredible game-high 61 minutes and scored 34 points in Portland's 140–139 loss, in which five players each logged 50 or more minutes.

There was enough drama for four games. Capping his team's 12–3 run over the final 1:34, Portland's Arvydas Sabonis hit a leaning three-pointer with 2.7 seconds left in regulation to tie the score at 98 and signal the beginning of the seemingly endless end.

The Blazers seemed to be in command in the second and third overtimes. But the Suns erased a 119–116 deficit with 7.1 seconds left in the third extra session when Rex Chapman took an inbounds pass, whirled and drilled an off-balance 30-footer to retie the game at 119.

"It was the most exciting basketball game I have ever played in," said Isaiah Rider.

No wonder Rider got such a kick out of it. The Blazers' guard, who tied the Suns' Danny Manning for game scoring honors with 35 points, found there was time to squeeze off an incredible 36 field-goal attempts.

> **Gerald and Dominique Wilkins are the highest-scoring brother tandem in the NBA, with 37,884 points entering 1997–98.**

WALL-TO-WALL WILLIAMS

The following is an NBA All-Williams Team, including active players only, by position.

Walt Williams, small forward, Portland
Jayson Williams, power forward, New Jersey
Brian Williams, center, Detroit
Micheal Williams, guard, Minnesota
Alvin Williams, guard, Toronto

Reserves: Buck Williams, F, New York; Herb Williams, F, New York; Scott Williams, C, Philadelphia; Lorenzo Williams, C, Washington; Jerome Williams, F, Detroit; Travis Williams, F, Charlotte; Eric Williams, F, Denver; Monty Williams, F, San Antonio; John Williams, F-C, Phoenix; Aaron Williams, Seattle.

> **The reason why Chuck Person is known as "The Rifleman" is not because he comes out of the locker room shooting, even though he does. He is named Chuck Connors Person, after the baseball player and actor who starred in *The Rifleman* on television.**

ALL IN THE FAMILY

Don't think the ability to hit a jumper is in the genes? Consider the following list of current players with kin who have a history in the NBA or ABA.

Jon Barry, Brent Barry, and Drew Barry—sons of Rick
Kobe Bryant—son of Joe (Jellybean)
Shandon Anderson—brother of Willie
Hubert Davis—nephew of Walter Davis
Danny Ferry—son of Bob
Harvey Grant—twin brother of Horace
Charles Jones—brother of Caldwell, Major and Wil
Grant Long—nephew of John Long,
   cousin of Terry Mills
Danny Manning—son of Ed
Ed O'Bannon—brother of Charles
Wesley Person—brother of Chuck
Eric Piatkowski—son of Walt (ABA)
Rex Chapman—son of Wayne (ABA)
Brent Price—brother of Mark
Jalen Rose—son of Jimmy Walker
Dan Schayes—son of Dolph
David Vaughn III—son of David Jr. (ABA)
Gerald Wilkins—brother of Dominique

> Wilt Chamberlain averaged 48.5 minutes per game in 1961–62, because of overtime contests as he played 79 of 80 complete games, and he averaged 50.4 points per game.

> Popeye Jones got his nickname from his brother David, who happened to be watching that cartoon when his mother brought Popeye the baby home from the hospital.

MORE MAGIC

Kareem Abdul-Jabbar, averaging 35 points per game in the series, was back in Los Angeles with a sprained ankle, watching his Los Angeles Lakers team on television.

Earvin (Magic) Johnson, a 6-foot-9 rookie point guard, was asked by coach Paul Westhead to play point center against Darryl Dawkins and the powerful Philadelphia 76ers front line in Game 6 of the NBA Finals, May 16, 1980.

Magic filled in for Abdul-Jabbar, all right. In fact, the young sensation pulled the load for himself and the missing Kareem. Johnson turned in a remarkable 42-point, 15-rebound, seven-assist, three-steal, one-block performance as the Lakers closed out the Sixers, 123–107.

After being named the Finals MVP, Magic—only the third player in history to win NCAA and NBA titles back-to-back—wore his trademark wall-to-wall grin as he said to Kareem via TV, "Big fella, I did it for you. I know your ankle hurts, but I want you to get up and dance."

HAVLICEK STEALS THE BALL!

It was Game 7 of the Eastern Finals, April 15, 1965, at the Boston Garden, with the Celtics of Bill Russell (29 rebounds) and the Philadelphia 76ers of Wilt Chamberlain (30 points, 32 rebounds) locked in perhaps their most classic struggle.

However, ultimately, the show and the ball were stolen by the Celtics' remarkable sixth man, John Havlicek. Though he had a distinguished career, Hondo is remembered for a single moment—as eternally recorded by broadcaster Johnny Most: "Havlicek steals the ball. It's all over. It's all over!"

Russell's turnover gave Philly a final chance to erase a 110–109 Boston lead with five seconds left. But Havlicek, guarding Chet Walker, tipped away Hal Greer's inbounds pass in the general direction of Celtics teammate Sam Jones (37 points), who dribbled out the clock.

Boston went on to win the title by beating Los Angeles in the Finals for its seventh crown in eight seasons.

Nick Anderson wears No. 25 in honor of Ben Wilson, his friend and former prep teammate from Chicago who was tragically shot and killed.

- I was recognized as one of the 50 Greatest Players in NBA history and an 11-time NBA All-Star selection going into 1997–98.

- Born August 5, 1962, in Kingston, Jamaica, I came to the United States at age 11.

- As the first of a string of athletic Georgetown centers to leave their mark on the pros, I preceded my friends, Dikembe Mutombo and Alonzo Mourning, to the NBA.

- Better known for my shot-blocking and defensive intimidation than for my offensive game as a collegian, I moved into 18th place on the NBA all-time scoring list, passing Hal Greer, on November 4, 1996, and finished 1996–97 with 21,539 points on .513 career shooting for my first 12 pro seasons.

- I was the No. 1 overall pick in the 1985 NBA Draft and NBA Rookie of the Year in 1986, despite being utilized as a 7-foot power forward in a Twin Tower formation with Bill Cartwright.

- I was a member of United States Olympic teams that won gold medals in 1984 and 1992.

- I am the Knicks' all-time leading scorer (supplanting Walt Frazier), rebounder (9,513 coming into 1997–98), ball thief (979 career steals) and shot-blocker (2,516).

ANSWER:
MY NAME IS PATRICK EWING.

TRUE OR FALSE?

Wilt Chamberlain never fouled out in 1,205 regular-season and playoff games, scored 70 or more points in a regular-season game six times, scored 50 or more in a game 46 times in one season, became the only center to lead the NBA in assists in 1967–68, made more free throws in a game than anyone else in history (28).

ANSWER: All true.

MILLER TIME, AGAIN

On May 7, 1995, a little more than a year after his 25-point fourth-quarter tour de force and 39-point show had staggered the Knicks in the playoffs, the Indiana Pacers' Reggie Miller performed an encore—on the very same Madison Square Garden court.

In Game 1 of the Eastern Conference Semifinals, Miller personally erased a 105–99 deficit within the final 18.7 seconds.

Miller had missed 11 of his first 16 shots. However, in a span of just 8.9 seconds, he scored eight points. He made two three-point jumpers—the second following his interception of an Anthony Mason inbounds pass—and two free throws, with 7.5 seconds left. That capped a 31-point effort by Miller and provided the winning points in a 107–105 Indiana victory.

The Pacers won the series in seven games.

BEST NICKNAMES

These current NBA players are better known by their aliases.

Daron Oshay Blaylock	Mookie
Ronald Jerome Jones	Popeye
Vernell Eufay Coles	Bimbo
Glenn Robinson	Big Dog
Tyrone Bogues	Muggsy
Anfernee Hardaway	Penny
Armon Gilliam	The Hammer
Chuck Person	The Rifleman
Gary Payton	The Glove
Jerome Richardson Jr.	Pooh
Greg Anderson	Cadillac
Clyde Drexler	The Glide
Theodore Edwards	Blue
LaPhonso Ellis	The Fonz
Karl Malone	The Mailman
Shawn Kemp	Reign Man
Hakeem Olajuwon	The Dream
Bryant Reeves	Big Country
David Robinson	The Admiral
Dennis Rodman	Worm
Chris Whitney	Hawkeye
John Williams	Hot Rod
Mitch Richmond	Rock
Lionel Simmons	Train
Corliss Williamson	Big Nasty
Kevin Gamble	Oscar

PAXSON SENDS SUNS INTO ECLIPSE

It was a symbol of The Team of the Nineties' unflagging commitment to winning unselfishly and their unflappable nature at crunch time. It was a reminder of how well the Chicago Bulls' role players complemented Michael Jordan and Scottie Pippen. It was the trademark moment of a team that never forgot the ring was the thing.

And, for a change, it was not His Airness who knocked down the clutch shot that made the Bulls winners of their third straight championship. It was veteran John Paxson, who had averaged only 4.2 points per game during that regular season.

With the Suns leading 98–96 in Game 6 of the NBA Finals at America West Arena, June 20, 1993, and Charles Barkley's Suns on the brink of forcing a decisive seventh game, the Bulls patiently passed the ball around the perimeter. The other four Bulls had touched the ball before it finally landed in the hands of the wide-open Paxson. His three-point shot with 3.9 seconds left gave the Bulls their 99–98 triumph.

Teamwork at its best, when it mattered most.

> Priest Lauderdale, whose godfather is former Utah guard Rickey Green, was named after the Ron O'Neal character in the movie *Superfly*.

THE FORCE-OF-NATURE TEAM

Mother Nature has her share of creatures and features in the NBA ranks.

Rick Fox
Hersey (The Hawk) Hawkins
Joe Wolf
Horacio Llamas
Larry Bird
Bird Averitt
Otis Birdsong
Sonny Dove
Garfield Heard
Larry Finch
Harry (The Horse) Gallatin
Rory Sparrow
Calvin Natt
Glenn (Big Dog) Robinson
Dennis (Worm) Rodman
Matt Fish
Doc Rivers
Mike Gale
George McCloud
Jalen Rose
Shea Seals
Cherokee Parks
Tree Rollins
Adrian Branch
Scott Brooks
Kenny (Sky) Walker
Kenny Fields
Charles (Oak) Oakley
Brian Winters
Michael (Animal) Smith

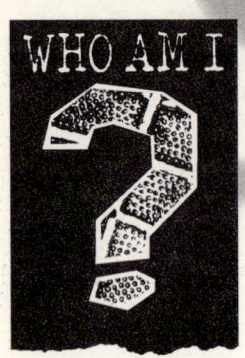

- Born June 22, 1962, in New Orleans, I grew up idolizing Arthur Ashe, Julius Erving and Walt Frazier.

- The University of Houston retired my No. 22.

- I hold the NBA record for most points scored in overtime in a playoff game with 13, vs. the Lakers, in Game 3 of the Western Conference first-round series, April 29, 1992.

- I was named to the All-Star team for a 10th straight season in 1996–97, but did not play because of injury.

- I was drafted 14th overall by Portland in 1983 and I served as that franchise's leading performer until being traded in February 1995. I remain the Trail Blazers' leading all-time scorer (18,040), rebounder (5,339) and assist leader (1,795).

- I went to the NBA Finals in 1990 and 1992 with Portland, but did not win a championship until after returning to Houston in 1995, when I averaged 20.5 points, 7.0 rebounds, 5.0 assists and 1.5 steals in the postseason.

- I entered the 1997–98 season as the 21st-ranked scorer in NBA history with 20,908 points and I was ranked fifth all-time in steals with 2,081.

ANSWER: MY NAME IS CLYDE DREXLER.

WORKING OVERTIME

The following NBA players, past and present, have names that suggest they have other activities to keep them busy if their basketball careers falter.

Haywoode Workman
Mitchell Butler
Anthony Peeler
Vin Baker
Anthony Mason
Karl (The Mailman) Malone
Mark Pope
Terry Porter
Derek Fisher
Lindsey Hunter
Andrew DeClercq
Johnny Taylor
Tony Farmer
Reggie Miller
Jim Brewer
Donnie Butcher

> **Dennis Rodman, who decided he wanted to play basketball at the age of 20, earned his nickname "Worm" for the way he used to squirm as a child while playing pinball.**

WEST'S PRAYER IS ANSWERED, SORT OF

Jerry West was 60 feet from the basket, but he let fly anyway. It was not like he had any choice. His Los Angeles Lakers were down by two points, and the final seconds were ticking off Game 3 of the 1970 NBA Finals against the Knicks, April 29, 1970, at the Forum.

The Knicks' Walt Frazier remembered thinking, "The man is crazy. He looks determined. He thinks it is really going in."

Swish.

Dave DeBusschere, a Knick forward, collapsed to the court under the basket as if he had been shot as his legs surrendered to the shock.

Because this game preceded the introduction of the three-point shot to the NBA, the game was tied. And the Knicks somehow regrouped to win it in overtime, 111–108.

"It was a beautiful thing wasted," said West of his remarkable bomb.

> Michael Jordan wears his University of North Carolina shorts under his Bulls uniform for good luck.

WHO AM I

● While I am thought of primarily as a scorer, with a career mark of 24.2 points per game through my first 14 pro seasons, I led the NBA in blocked shots in 1990 (4.59 per game), 1991 (3.95) and 1993 (4.17) en route to the league's top career total in rejections (3,363, going into 1997–98).

● I was discovered on the soccer fields of Lagos, Nigeria, in the days when all I wanted to do was be a goaltender. I didn't start playing basketball until 1978.

● Along with current teammate and friend Clyde Drexler, I was a charter member of Phi Slama Jama at the University of Houston. The school went 88–16 in three seasons and reached the NCAA Finals three times during my time there.

● Teamed with 7-foot-4 Ralph Sampson, I was part of the Twin Tower front line that carried the Rockets to the NBA Finals in 1985–86.

● I am the first player in history to be named NBA MVP, Defensive Player of the Year and NBA Finals MVP in one season, a feat I accomplished in 1993–94 after leading the Rockets past the Knicks for the title.

● I won the NBA Finals MVP honors a second-straight time in 1995, after fueling a series sweep over the Orlando Magic.

● My nickname is The Dream and my signature move is the Dream Shake, a nifty drop step, fake and spin move that makes defenders look silly.

ANSWER: MY NAME IS HAKEEM OLAJUWON.

NBA'S TRAVELING TEAM

These players are always on the move.

Danny Ferry
Antoine Carr
Antoine Walker
Neal Walk
Cadillac Anderson
Isaiah Rider
Terry Cummings
Sam Mack
Rodrick Rhodes
Chris Ford
Lionel (Train) Simmons
Leonard (Truck) Robinson
John (Hot Rod) Williams
Hot Rod Hundley
Mike Sojourner
Bill Bridges
Albert Ferrari

Vlade Divac's 1989 wedding in Yugoslavia was televised nationally.

LAST FIVE NBA ROOKIES OF THE YEAR

1996–97	Allen Iverson, Philadelphia 76ers
1995–96	Damon Stoudamire, Toronto Raptors
1994–95	Grant Hill, Detroit Pistons, and Jason Kidd, Dallas Mavericks
1993–94	Chris Webber, Golden State Warriors
1992–93	Shaquille O'Neal, Orlando Magic

Scott Burrell was a first-round pick of the Seattle Mariners in 1989 as a pitcher, but opted to attend the University of Connecticut to play basketball.

Which player averaged a triple-double in points, assists and rebounds for a season?

A. Grant Hill
B. Scottie Pippen
C. Anfernee Hardaway
D. Jerry West
E. Oscar Robertson

ANSWER: Oscar Robertson, known as the Big O, averaged a triple-double in his second pro season, with the Cincinnati Royals in 1961–62: 30.8 points, 11.4 assists and 12.5 rebounds per game.

A.C. GREEN KEEPS ON TICKING

As NBA power forwards go these days, A. C. Green is a relatively undersized 6-foot-9, 225 pounds, an almost frail-looking specimen who bangs heads with giants every night. Other power forwards have drawn more attention, scored more, rebounded more.

But Green has done one thing that no other NBA player has ever done: He owns the longest consecutive-game streak in league history.

Green became the NBA's answer to Cal Ripken Jr. when he passed Randy Smith's mark of 906 consecutive-game appearances (1972–83), with No. 907 on the night of November 20, 1997, when Green's Dallas Mavericks hosted Golden State. Among those on hand for A.C.'s record-setting game were Ripken, baseball's all-time iron man, ex-Laker teammate James Worthy, Randy Smith and Green's parents.

When the streak began November 9, 1986, there was no reason to think an 11-year run had begun. But Green played through fatigue, food poisoning, torn ligaments, muscle cramps and sprained ankles. Wearing a plastic mask the night after he had suffered cracked teeth courtesy of an elbow from J. R. Reid in 1996, Green managed to play 68 seconds.

"The injuries have been what I would characterize as fender benders—nothing more serious that that, so I have been fortunate," said Green. "And God plays a tremendous part. When I don't think I can go, He tells me I can."

LAST FIVE NBA MVPs (regular season)

1996–97	Karl Malone, Utah Jazz
1995–96	Michael Jordan, Chicago Bulls
1994–95	David Robinson, San Antonio Spurs
1993–94	Hakeem Olajuwon, Houston Rockets
1992–93	Charles Barkley, Phoenix Suns

Terry Cummings, an ordained minister, performed the ceremony when Sean Elliott married Akiko Herron, September 4, 1993.

Allen Iverson was drafted No. 1 overall by the Philadelphia 76ers in 1996, becoming the first guard to be so designated since:

A. Magic Johnson
B. John Lucas
C. Walt Frazier
D. Grant Hill
E. Anfernee Hardaway

ANSWER: Magic Johnson was chosen first overall by the Lakers in 1979. After that, forwards and centers were the top picks for the next 17 years until Iverson came along. Lucas was taken No. 1 overall in 1976. Among the centers chosen No. 1 were Joe Barry Carroll, Ralph Sampson and Pervis Ellison.

WHO AM I

- Just short of my 21st birthday, I won NBA Rookie of the Year honors in 1993.

- I played with Chris Jackson (now known as Mahmoud Abdul-Rauf) and Stanley Roberts at Louisiana State, averaging 27.6 points on .628 shooting along with 14.7 rebounds and 5.0 blocks per game as a sophomore in 1990–91.

- I was chosen with the first pick overall in the 1992 NBA draft by the Orlando Magic.

- A whopping 322 of my 743 baskets as a rookie were dunks.

- I won gold medals at the 1994 World Championship of Basketball, where I was named MVP, and at the 1996 Olympics.

- After being edged out for a scoring crown by David Robinson in the final game of the 1993–94 season, I won my first scoring crown by averaging 29.3 points for the Magic in 1994–95, and helped carry that team to the NBA Finals.

- I delighted Jack Nicholson, Arsenio Hall and Dyan Cannon when I signed with the Los Angeles Lakers as a free agent before the 1996–97 season.

ANSWER: MY NAME IS SHAQUILLE RASHAUN O'NEAL.

The highest field-goal percentage by an NBA player in any regular season was recorded by:

A. Michael Jordan
B. Wilt Chamberlain
C. Shaquille O'Neal
D. Jerry West
E. Artis Gilmore

ANSWER: Wilt Chamberlain shot an outrageous .727 from the floor for the 1972–73 Los Angeles Lakers, and it marked the ninth and final time in which he led the league in that category. The next closest league-leading mark belonged to Artis Gilmore at .670 for the Chicago Bulls in 1980–81. Though he had nine scoring titles to his credit coming into 1997–98, Michael Jordan has never led the league in field-goal accuracy.

> **Tim Duncan routinely wore his practice shorts backward at Wake Forest.**

Which player holds the NBA record for most championship rings?

A. Magic Johnson
B. Michael Jordan
C. Bill Russell
D. Shaquille O'Neal
E. Larry Bird

ANSWER: Bill Russell won 11 titles with the Boston Celtics from 1956–57 through 1968–69.

IS THERE A DOCTOR IN THE HOUSE?

The Atlanta Hawks' Alan Henderson, a graduate of Indiana with a B.A. in biology, has been accepted to medical school and intends to attend after his NBA playing career is over.

He won't be the first doctor to come out of the NBA ranks. There was also Dr. Ernie Vandeweghe, the former Knick great and father of layman (or layup man) Kiki. And there was Dr. J—but Julius Erving got his Ph.D. for operating on opponents on the basketball court.

> Brian Williams' father Tony was an original member of the 1950s singing group The Platters.

The player who notched the NBA's highest assist average for a regular season is:

A. Magic Johnson
B. Lenny Wilkens
C. John Stockton
D. Maurice Cheeks
E. Isiah Thomas

ANSWER: In the midst of stringing together nine straight assist crowns, John Stockton averaged 14.5 for the Utah Jazz in 1989–90, eclipsing Isiah Thomas' record of 13.98 for the Detroit Pistons in 1984–85.

Match the players with the colleges they attended:

Scottie Pippen   Virginia Union
John Stockton   Louisiana Tech
Karl Malone   American International
Joe Dumars   Gonzaga
Mario Elie   Hartford
Vin Baker   McNeese State
Charles Oakley   Central Arkansas

ANSWERS: Pippen/Central Arkansas; Stockton/Gonzaga; Malone/Louisiana Tech; Dumars/McNeese State; Elie/American International; Baker/Hartford; Oakley/Virginia Union.

WHAT'S IN A NAME?

Here is a list of the highest-scoring Johnsons in NBA history (regular season):

Player	Total	Average
1. Eddie A. Johnson	18,557	16.6
2. Magic Johnson	17,707	19.5
3. Dennis Johnson	15,535	14.1
4. Marques Johnson	13,892	20.1
5. Vinnie Johnson	11,825	12.0

Kevin Gamble wears No. 35 in honor of his late former Boston Celtics' teammate, Reggie Lewis.

WILT SCORES 100!

Only 4,124 people were on hand that night in Hershey, Pennsylvania, for a late-season game between the Philadelphia Warriors and the New York Knicks. But thousands more would claim they were there on March 2, 1962, the night that Wilt Chamberlain burned the Knicks for an NBA-record 100 points.

The Big Dipper scored 23 points in the first quarter, 18 in the second, 28 in the third and 31 points in the fourth quarter. He reached the 100-point mark with 46 seconds left, on a basket that gave the Warriors a 169–146 lead—and then the small crowd of fans swarmed the court.

Wilt wound up taking 63 of the Warriors' 115 field-goal attempts, making 36 of them. More impressively, Chamberlain—notorious for his poor foul-shooting—converted 28 of his 32 attempts from the charity stripe.

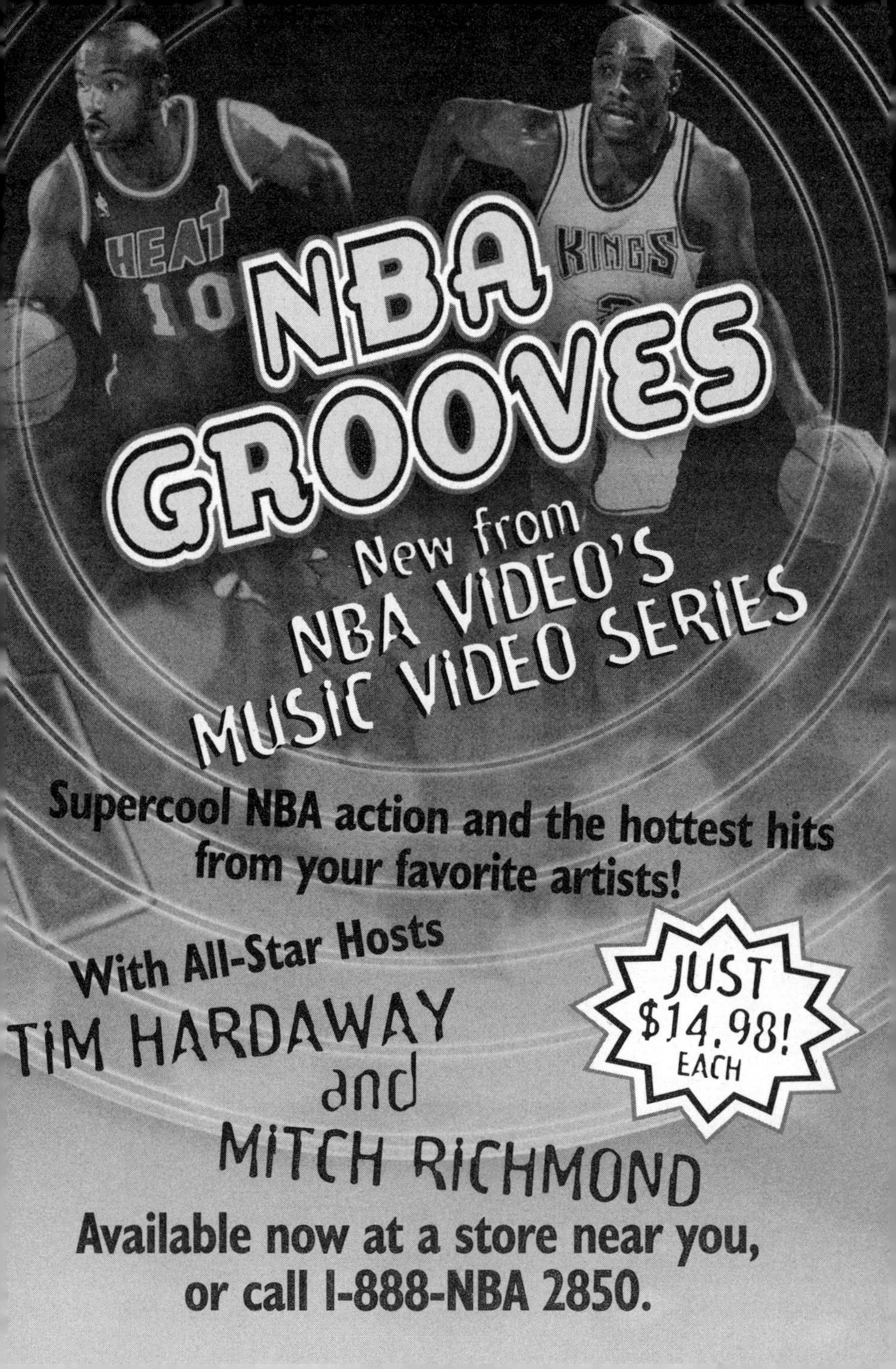
HEAT
10
KINGS
NBA
GROOVES
New from
NBA VIDEO'S
MUSIC VIDEO SERIES
Supercool NBA action and the hottest hits from your favorite artists!
With All-Star Hosts
TIM HARDAWAY
and
MITCH RICHMOND
JUST $14.98! EACH
Available now at a store near you, or call 1-888-NBA 2850.